T0012931

THE MET

DK

Mystery at the Museum

BY
HELEN FRIEL

Hello, my name is 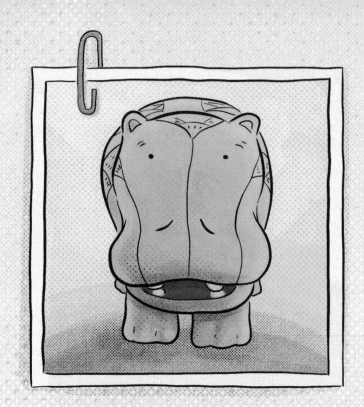. These are the hieroglyphs that mean "hippopotamus." My nickname is William. Today, I live on Fifth Avenue in the middle of New York City. Specifically, in the Egyptian Art galleries of the famous Metropolitan Museum of Art. You might wonder how such a small hippo traveled all the way from Egypt to America ...

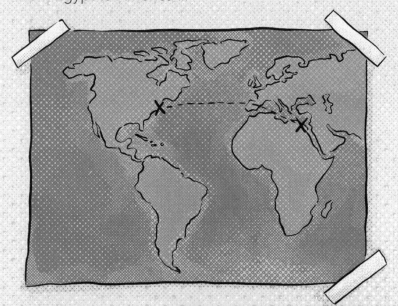

My story started around 4,000 years ago on the banks of the mighty Nile River in Africa. The Egyptian people met a lot of my big brothers and sisters while sailing in their boats on the Nile. I think of myself as a very kind hippo, but real ones can be extremely grumpy if you catch them at the wrong moment.

Egyptians believed in rebirth after death. Little hippos, like me, were placed inside tombs to help the person who had died to be rejuvenated and reborn. I was made in a striking blue color from a ceramic material called faience and painted with drawings of lotus flowers. Lotus flowers can be found in the Nile. They close at night and reopen in the morning. They were seen as a symbol of rejuvenation.

The Egyptians admired the strength of hippos, but they were also afraid of them, as hippos can be dangerous. To keep me from being a danger to anyone three of my legs were broken off before I was placed inside the tomb. I'm a friendly hippo, but I guess they didn't know that! I lived in the tomb for a long, long time. It was very dark and quiet. I didn't mind too much. I passed the time by singing to myself.

Over 100 years ago in 1910, things changed. Suddenly, my dark and quiet home was full of light and archeologists shouting to one another. They were very happy to see me. Once I left the tomb, I had a few different homes. I was cleaned and given three new legs! People came to visit me once in a while, and I enjoyed showing off my gleaming blue color to everyone who stopped by.

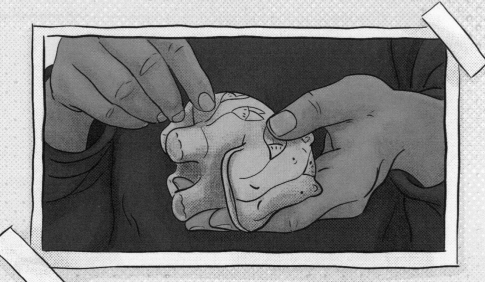

In 1917, I arrived at The Metropolitan Museum of Art in bustling New York City where thousands of people visit me every day! In 1931, a man named Captain H. M. Raleigh gave me my nickname. He wrote in an article for *Punch* magazine that his family owned a picture of me in their home. He said that whenever his family had to make a tricky decision, they would ask my advice. The Raleigh family had nicknamed me William, and it stuck.

Ninjin is my best friend. She is a rabbit from Japan. When I arrived at the Museum, Ninjin showed me around and introduced me to everyone. She's very smart. If you need a puzzle solved, Ninjin is your rabbit!

I have lived in the Egyptian galleries at The Met for over 100 years! But when the visitors go home, I love wandering the Museum's wide hallways and meeting other amazing characters who have arrived from around the globe. I sometimes miss my Egyptian home near the Nile, but I have made lots of new friends here. Let me introduce you to some of them.

Filibert is a rooster and the loudest of all the animals. You can hear him coming from a long way away! He acts as the Museum's town crier. If news needs to get around, he's the one to ask.

'Alam Guman Gajraj is an elephant from India. His name means "the arrogant one of the earth, King of Elephants." He may be the king of the elephants but if you need help reaching something on a high shelf, 'Alam Guman will use his long trunk to help you out.

Ruby came to the Museum from Staffordshire, England. Some might say she's a touch dramatic, but I think she's the bravest cat in Manhattan. Occasionally she gets a little sad, but we love having her around.

Thank goodness you're here! We've got an emergency on our hands! For months the curators have been planning a special surprise exhibition. Everything seemed to be going well. The invitations to the opening had been sent and the floors had been swept.

The curators were ready to install the works of art. For this exhibition, loans had been sent from all over the world. Each one was carefully packed so that it arrived safely. There's one problem—the boxes are locked!

To keep the works of art super safe, the storage boxes can only be opened by solving the puzzle-lock on the front. The curators have tried but haven't solved a single one. And the opening is TOMORROW! It looks like we've got just one night to save this exhibition. If we can't get those boxes open, the gallery will be empty!

I've gathered the best puzzle-breaking team I know: Ninjin, 'Alam Guman, Ruby, and Filibert.

Each box can be opened by collecting three correct tokens from the Museum department listed on the label.

You can visit the departments in any order, but you'll need to visit all of them to open all of the boxes and find your way to the special exhibition.

How to begin:

1. Decide which department you'd like to visit and make a note of the map reference on the label.

2. Turn to the map on the next page and follow the instructions to start collecting tokens.

Good luck!

ASIAN ART

41M

Map Reference

UNLOCK

UNLOCK

EGYPTIAN ART

16M

Map Reference

 Grab a piece of paper or a notebook and write down the names of the galleries and map references. Keep track of the tokens you collect—each one has a number listed next to it on the next page for reference.

When you have unlocked all of the boxes, turn to the map page and follow the "Special Exhibition" instructions to make it to the opening!

The Met is a big place. To find each department you want to visit, you'll need to use the map on page 9, opposite.

How to collect tokens:

1. Find the map reference for the department you want to visit on the boxes in the storeroom on pages 6 and 7, then look at the map. Use the reference to find the page number for the department. Read along the numbers and up the letters to find the right square.

2. Turn to the page number and you'll find yourself in a gallery. Read the map carefully or you might get lost!

3. From the gallery, visit three objects and collect a token from each. Pick an object and go to the page number on its information label.

4. Solve the puzzles to collect tokens. Keep track of the tokens you collect in a notebook.

5. Once you have collected the three tokens for each department, return to the storeroom, pick another department, and repeat!

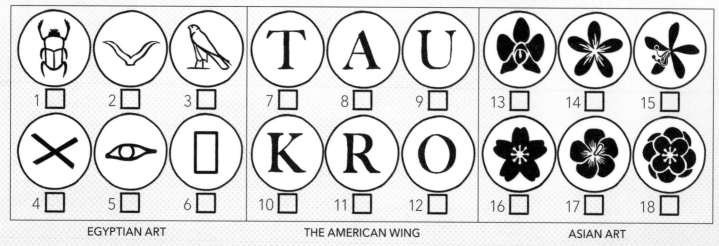

1 •	2 •	3 •
4	5 •	6
7 •	8	9 •

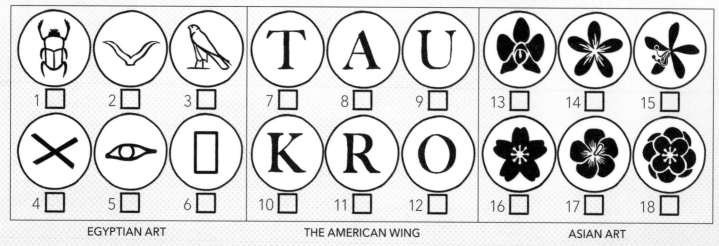

EGYPTIAN ART

THE AMERICAN WING

ASIAN ART

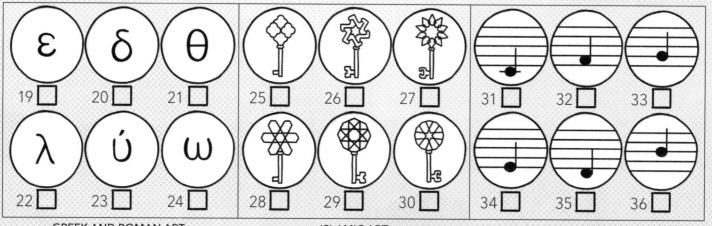

GREEK AND ROMAN ART

ISLAMIC ART

MUSICAL INSTRUMENTS

Have you found all of the tokens? Three from each department? Amazing! Let's get to the special exhibition in time for the opening.

◆ Each token you have collected has a number next to it. Add up the numbers of all 18 tokens (you might need a calculator!). Now match the number to one of the grid references on the invitation.

◆ Find the special exhibition by turning to the page number at the correct grid reference. Let's go!

Special Exhibition Invitation

You are invited to The Met's mystery exhibition. The exhibition can be found at one of the map references below ...

337	33H		437	33E		237	29F

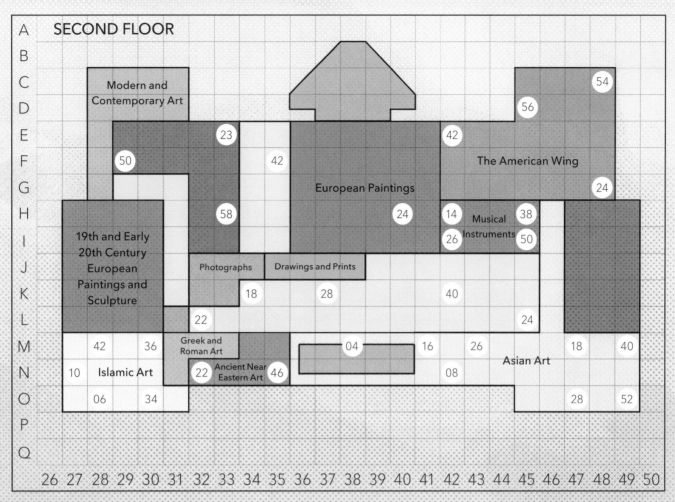

SECOND FLOOR

Modern and Contemporary Art

19th and Early 20th Century European Paintings and Sculpture

European Paintings

The American Wing

Musical Instruments

Photographs

Drawings and Prints

Islamic Art

Greek and Roman Art

Ancient Near Eastern Art

Asian Art

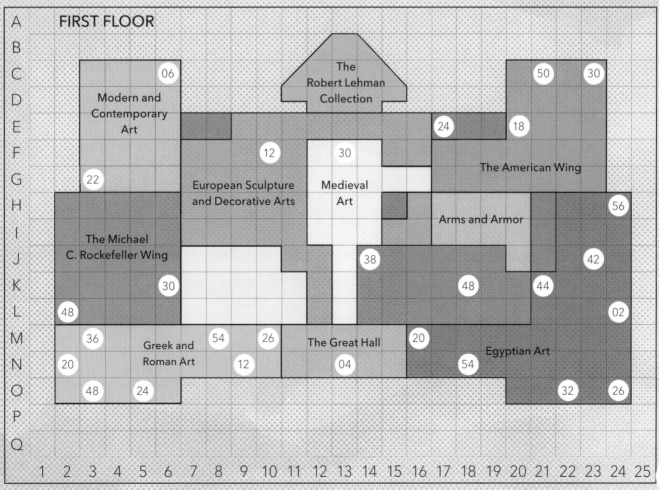

FIRST FLOOR

Modern and Contemporary Art

The Robert Lehman Collection

The American Wing

The Michael C. Rockefeller Wing

European Sculpture and Decorative Arts

Medieval Art

Arms and Armor

Greek and Roman Art

The Great Hall

Egyptian Art

WELCOME TO THE MET

This is the **Islamic Art** gallery. It is full of beautiful patterns and colors. The objects are from across the world—Morocco, Egypt, Turkey, Iran, Indonesia ... I could go on and on but there simply isn't time. We have to visit many works of art to be able to crack the puzzle lock. Careful, 'Alam Guman! Everything in The Met is very precious. Now, where shall we go first?

Decide which object you'd like to visit and check the information label to see which page you need to turn to.

INCENSE BURNER OF AMIR SAIF AL-DUNYA WA'L-DIN IBN MUHAMMAD AL-MAWARDI

DATE MADE: A.H. 577/1181–82 C.E.
COUNTRY OF ORIGIN: IRAN

This fantastical feline animal incense burner is over 35 in tall! It is covered in patterns and Arabic calligraphy. The calligraphy includes the name of the artist and the person who commissioned the art. The head comes off so that incense could be placed inside. As the incense burned it would make your home smell delightful!

PAGE 34

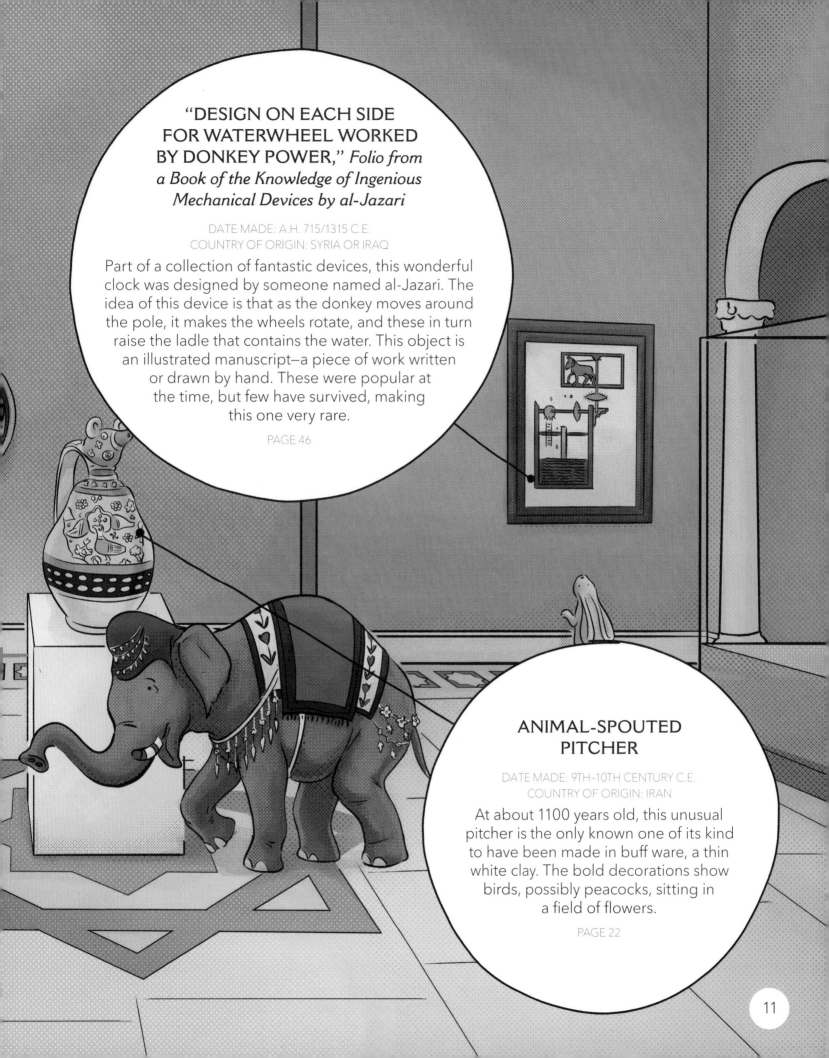

"DESIGN ON EACH SIDE FOR WATERWHEEL WORKED BY DONKEY POWER," *Folio from a Book of the Knowledge of Ingenious Mechanical Devices by al-Jazari*

DATE MADE: A.H. 715/1315 C.E.
COUNTRY OF ORIGIN: SYRIA OR IRAQ

Part of a collection of fantastic devices, this wonderful clock was designed by someone named al-Jazari. The idea of this device is that as the donkey moves around the pole, it makes the wheels rotate, and these in turn raise the ladle that contains the water. This object is an illustrated manuscript—a piece of work written or drawn by hand. These were popular at the time, but few have survived, making this one very rare.

PAGE 46

ANIMAL-SPOUTED PITCHER

DATE MADE: 9TH–10TH CENTURY C.E.
COUNTRY OF ORIGIN: IRAN

At about 1100 years old, this unusual pitcher is the only known one of its kind to have been made in buff ware, a thin white clay. The bold decorations show birds, possibly peacocks, sitting in a field of flowers.

PAGE 22

We're here-ere-ere-ere-ere-ere! Wow, listen to that echo-o-o-o-o-o! This spectacular space is the **Greek and Roman Art** gallery. Just look at all those columns! Lots of different cultures contributed to this gallery. Not only the ancient Greeks and Romans, but also people like the Minoans, Mycenaeans, and Etruscans, who lived even further in the past. That floor looks like it would be perfect for sliding on, but we've got an exhibition to save. Remember, we need to get a token from each work of art here. Who shall we visit first?

Decide which object you'd like to visit and check the information label to see which page you need to turn to.

ZOOMORPHIC VESSELS

DATE MADE: BETWEEN CA. 1725 B.C.E. AND 3RD CENTURY C.E.
CULTURE: ROMAN AND CYPRIOT

These three quirky vessels might look similar but they span a huge time period and come from different places. One is thought to represent a deer and another a mouse. The third is a mystery animal with lots of character!

PAGE 48

MARBLE STATUE OF A LION

DATE MADE: CA. 400–390 B.C.E.
CULTURE: GREEK

This fierce-looking marble lion was built to guard tombs. Although it started its life in Greece, it was eventually taken to Rome.

PAGE 36

TERRACOTTA DINOS (MIXING BOWL)

DATE MADE: CA. 630–615 B.C.E.
CULTURE: GREEK

This beautiful mixing bowl comes from Corinth. It was designed to hold wine that was mixed with water. This was drunk at parties that took place after a meal. The top half of this bowl is decorated with sphinxes (mythical creatures with the head of a woman and the body of a lion) and panthers. The bottom half also includes lions and goats.

PAGE 24

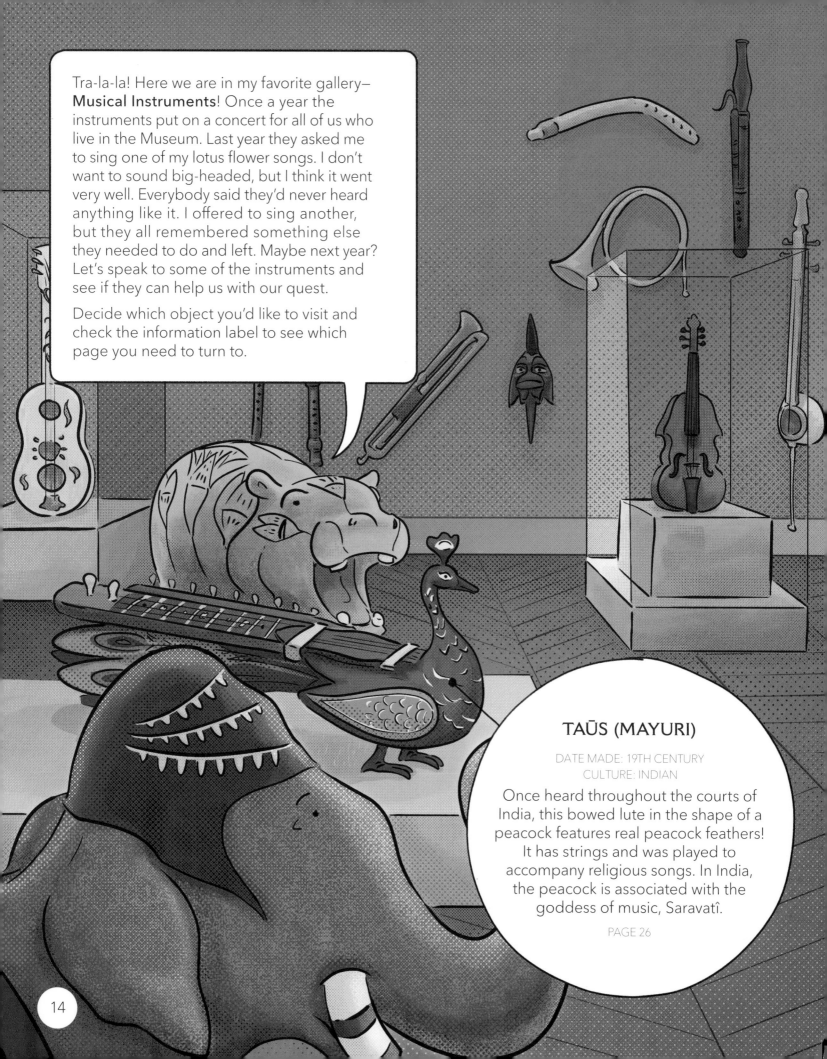

Tra-la-la! Here we are in my favorite gallery— **Musical Instruments**! Once a year the instruments put on a concert for all of us who live in the Museum. Last year they asked me to sing one of my lotus flower songs. I don't want to sound big-headed, but I think it went very well. Everybody said they'd never heard anything like it. I offered to sing another, but they all remembered something else they needed to do and left. Maybe next year? Let's speak to some of the instruments and see if they can help us with our quest.

Decide which object you'd like to visit and check the information label to see which page you need to turn to.

TAŪS (MAYURI)

DATE MADE: 19TH CENTURY
CULTURE: INDIAN

Once heard throughout the courts of India, this bowed lute in the shape of a peacock features real peacock feathers! It has strings and was played to accompany religious songs. In India, the peacock is associated with the goddess of music, Saravatî.

PAGE 26

O-DAIKO

DATE MADE: CA. 1873
CULTURE: JAPANESE

The o-daiko is a drum played in Japanese temples, at festivals, and during theatre performances. This particular drum is a symbol of peace and it has never been sounded. The story behind it tells of a drum that stood at a village gate, ready to be sounded if there was an attack. But through years of peace, it was never used, and hens and roosters began to live in it!

PAGE 38

DOUBLE WHISTLE

DATE MADE: 7TH–9TH CENTURY
CULTURE: MAYA

The Maya lived in what is now modern-day Mexico and Central America. They made this whistle in the form of a bird from pottery. It has two chambers. Blow through the tail for one sound and into a mouthpiece behind the ears for another. A small hole on the front of the bird can be covered to change the note of the lower chamber.

PAGE 50

The **Asian Art** department is unique in the Museum. Its collection covers 5,000 years and half the world's population. Imagine how many stories there are here! Let's see what we can find out as we travel through the galleries.

Decide which object you'd like to visit and check the information label to see which page you need to turn to.

BOX DECORATED WITH AUSPICIOUS SYMBOLS

DATE MADE: 19TH CENTURY
CULTURE: KOREAN

This wooden box is decorated with thin sheets of ox horn painted in bright colors. The box is covered in animals that symbolize different things, including good fortune and protection.

PAGE 52

JAR WITH WINGED ANIMALS OVER WAVES

DATE MADE: MID-15TH CENTURY
CULTURE: CHINESE

You don't often see a horse, an elephant, a mongoose, a fish, a rabbit, and two deer in one place. Even less often with wings! This extraordinary jar is thought to have been inspired by some of the amazing sea voyages of the Chinese fleet.

PAGE 40

RABBIT

DATE MADE: MID-19TH CENTURY
CULTURE: JAPANESE

This adorable rabbit is a netsuke. Netsukes are small, carved ornaments, used as toggles in traditional Japanese clothing. In Japanese folklore, a rabbit lives on the moon. In the tale, the rabbit helps the Man in the Moon and is rewarded by being taken there. The rabbit spends its time making mochi, a Japanese snack, made from rice.

PAGE 28

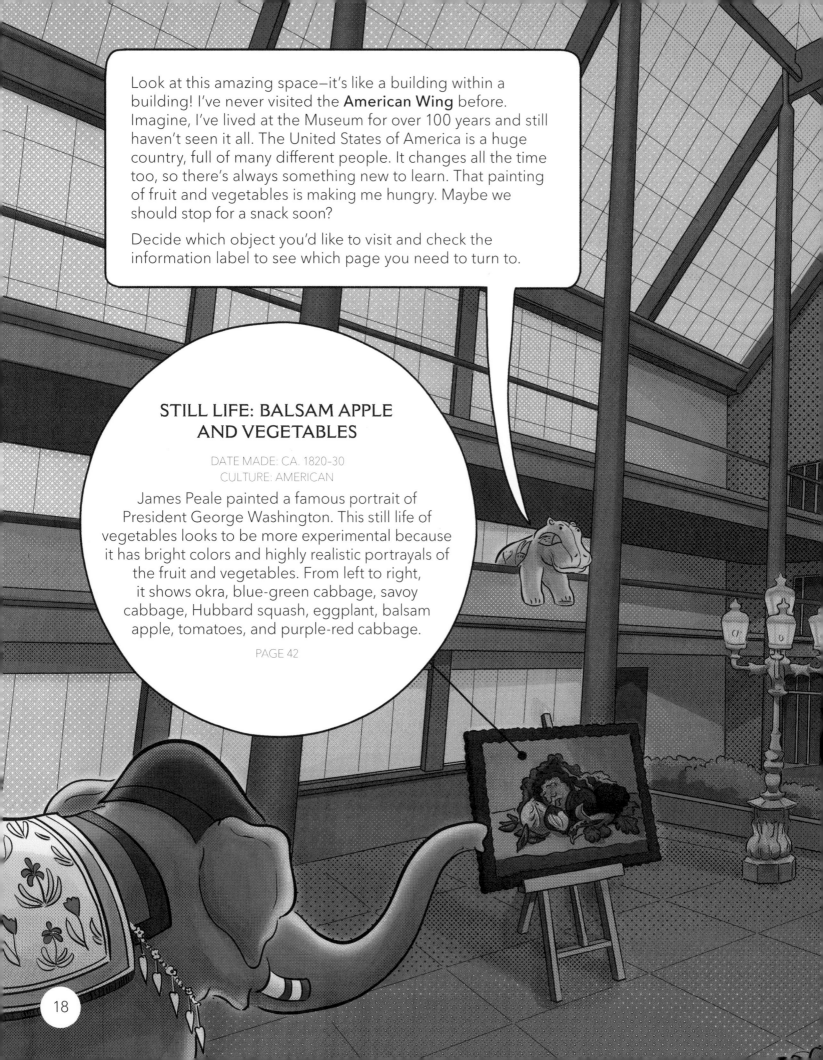

Look at this amazing space—it's like a building within a building! I've never visited the **American Wing** before. Imagine, I've lived at the Museum for over 100 years and still haven't seen it all. The United States of America is a huge country, full of many different people. It changes all the time too, so there's always something new to learn. That painting of fruit and vegetables is making me hungry. Maybe we should stop for a snack soon?

Decide which object you'd like to visit and check the information label to see which page you need to turn to.

STILL LIFE: BALSAM APPLE AND VEGETABLES

DATE MADE: CA. 1820-30
CULTURE: AMERICAN

James Peale painted a famous portrait of President George Washington. This still life of vegetables looks to be more experimental because it has bright colors and highly realistic portrayals of the fruit and vegetables. From left to right, it shows okra, blue-green cabbage, savoy cabbage, Hubbard squash, eggplant, balsam apple, tomatoes, and purple-red cabbage.

PAGE 42

SOCORRO BLACK-ON-WHITE
STORAGE JAR

DATE MADE: CA. 1050-1100
CULTURE: ANCESTRAL PUEBLO, NATIVE AMERICAN

This ancient storage jar was made to hold water by Pueblo potters who lived in the southwestern United States. Water remains an important resource to them in a very arid environment. The jar's black and white decoration likely represents the water circulating underneath the earth and falling from the sky.

PAGE 54

FIGURE OF A LION

DATE MADE: 1845-55
CULTURE: AMERICAN

This playful lion was made from clay by potter John Bell. The Bell family of potters were well known and produced lots of different pieces including flowerpots, pitchers, and cooking pots. It's thought that this lion is a special piece because it was kept by the Bell family, instead of being sold.

PAGE 30

BOOK OF THE DEAD
FOR NAUNY

DATE MADE: CA. 1050 B.C.E.
CULTURE: EGYPTIAN

Books of the Dead were manuscripts buried with ancient Egyptians. They contained spells and prayers that were believed to help the dead reach the afterlife. This one was created for Nauny, the daughter of a king, who died in her 70s. Unrolled, the scroll is more than 16 ft long! In this scroll, Nauny is facing judgment from Osiris, god of the underworld, to decide whether she has lived a life that the gods think is worthy of an eternal afterlife. The balanced scales show that she has lived a moral life and is worthy.

PAGE 56

FIGURE OF A BABOON

DATE MADE: CA. 600 B.C.E.
CULTURE: EGYPTIAN

The ancient Egyptians often associated animals with gods. Thoth, the god of writing, accounting, and learning was represented as an ibis (a long-legged wading bird) or a baboon. Like William, this baboon is faience, which means he is made of a ceramic material that has been decorated with an opaque colored glaze.

PAGE 44

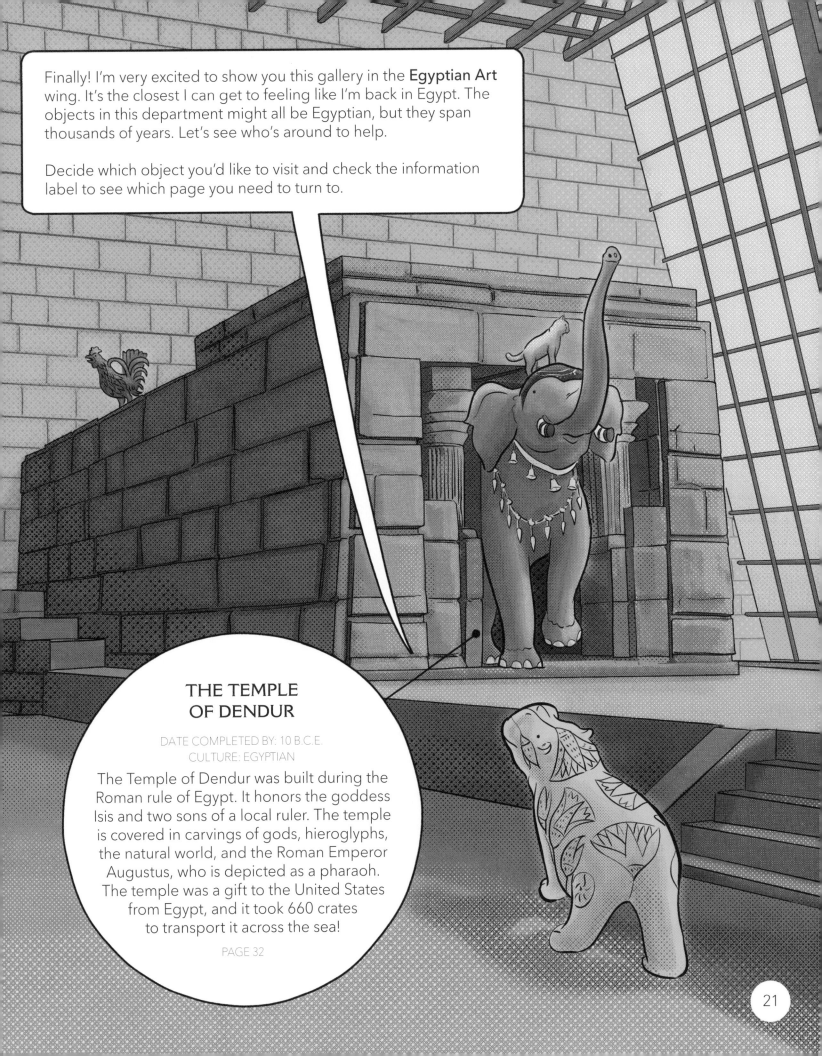

Finally! I'm very excited to show you this gallery in the **Egyptian Art** wing. It's the closest I can get to feeling like I'm back in Egypt. The objects in this department might all be Egyptian, but they span thousands of years. Let's see who's around to help.

Decide which object you'd like to visit and check the information label to see which page you need to turn to.

THE TEMPLE OF DENDUR

DATE COMPLETED BY: 10 B.C.E.
CULTURE: EGYPTIAN

The Temple of Dendur was built during the Roman rule of Egypt. It honors the goddess Isis and two sons of a local ruler. The temple is covered in carvings of gods, hieroglyphs, the natural world, and the Roman Emperor Augustus, who is depicted as a pharaoh. The temple was a gift to the United States from Egypt, and it took 660 crates to transport it across the sea!

PAGE 32

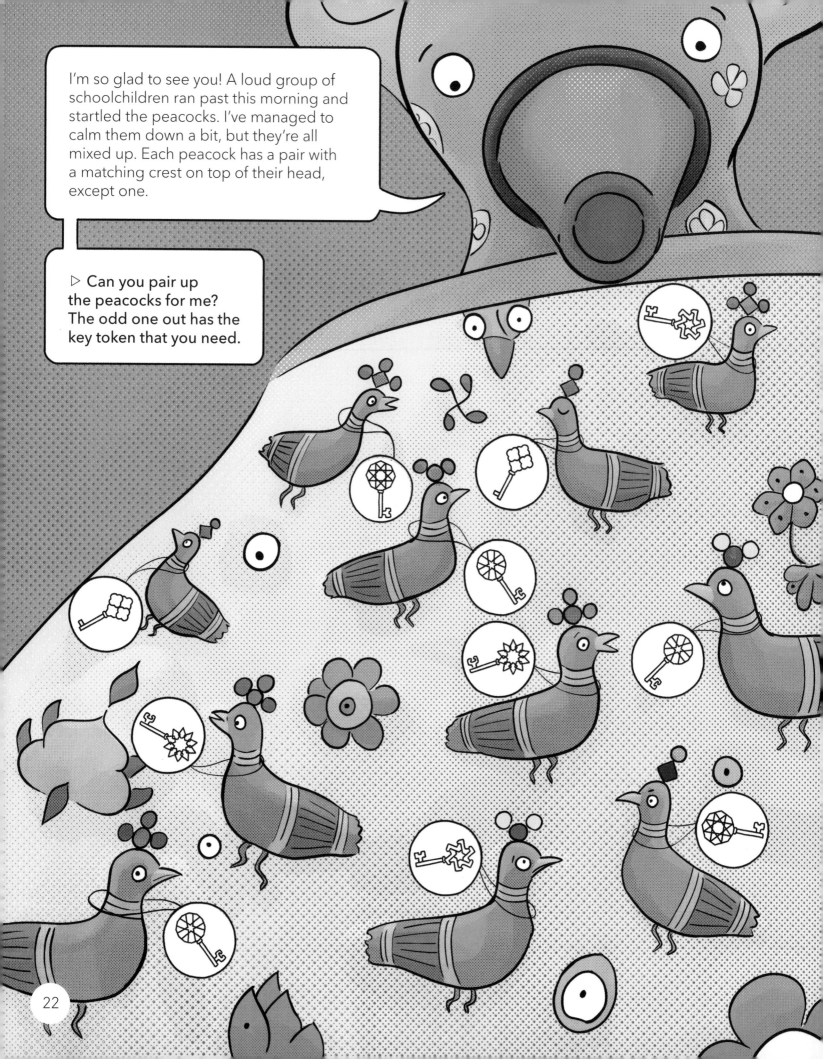

I'm so glad to see you! A loud group of schoolchildren ran past this morning and startled the peacocks. I've managed to calm them down a bit, but they're all mixed up. Each peacock has a pair with a matching crest on top of their head, except one.

▷ Can you pair up the peacocks for me? The odd one out has the key token that you need.

It's unusual to see such ... delicious-looking animals in these parts. I haven't tried hippo for a very long time.

Well, I suppose you could help with something that's been bothering us. Our bowl is covered with colorful symbols. We're very proud of how sharp they look. But someone got overexcited and knocked some of them off.

▷ We know that the same logic applies through the whole pattern. Look at the pattern and figure out which symbols from the options below go in the empty squares. When you know which symbol goes in the blue square, collect the corresponding token from the table.

MYSTERY TUNE

KEY

Western Notation	C	D	E	F	G	A	B	C
Western Sounds	do	re	mi	fa	sol	la	ti	do
Indian Svaras	Sa	Re	Ga	Ma	Pa	Dha	Ni	Sa
Animal								

Twinkle, Twinkle, Little Star
x2 x0 x3
x2 x2 x2 x3

Old MacDonald Had a Farm
x2 x2 x0
x2 x2 x0 x4

Row, Row, Row Your Boat
x0 x0 x3
x2 x3 x1 x1

Yankee Doodle
x3 x3 x0
x1 x0 x1 x6

Tra-la-la-la. No, wait. Tra-la-la-la-la. Nope! It's no good, I can't figure out this tune. Are any of you good at reading music?

You're in luck! I like to consider myself something of a musician. If we can lend a hand, could you help us find the token that we need?

Gladly—if you can figure out this song! In Indian music notation each sound or svara is associated with an animal that makes a similar noise. The mystery tune is written in Western notation. Can you translate the Western notes into svaras and figure out which song it is?

▷ 1. Look at the key and translate the Western notes of the mystery tune into the animal symbols.

▷ 2. Count how many of each animal symbol are in the tune.

▷ 3. Look at the four options and figure out the name of the mystery tune.

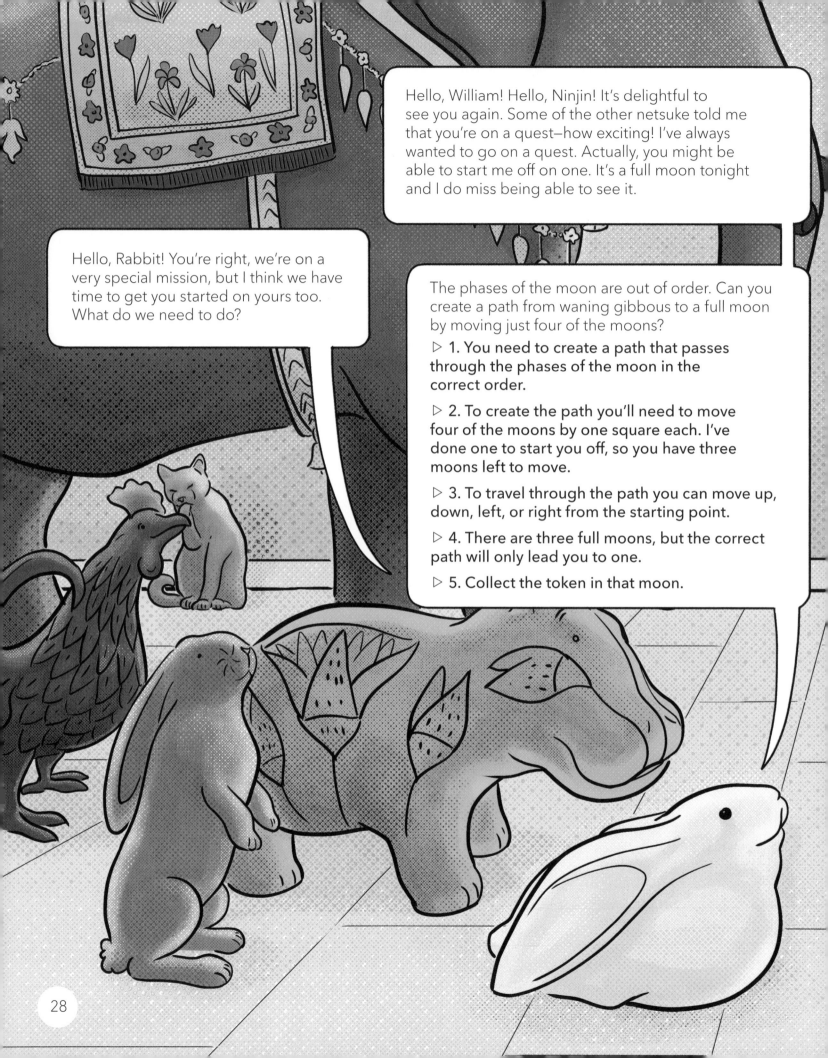

Hello, William! Hello, Ninjin! It's delightful to see you again. Some of the other netsuke told me that you're on a quest—how exciting! I've always wanted to go on a quest. Actually, you might be able to start me off on one. It's a full moon tonight and I do miss being able to see it.

Hello, Rabbit! You're right, we're on a very special mission, but I think we have time to get you started on yours too. What do we need to do?

The phases of the moon are out of order. Can you create a path from waning gibbous to a full moon by moving just four of the moons?

▷ 1. You need to create a path that passes through the phases of the moon in the correct order.

▷ 2. To create the path you'll need to move four of the moons by one square each. I've done one to start you off, so you have three moons left to move.

▷ 3. To travel through the path you can move up, down, left, or right from the starting point.

▷ 4. There are three full moons, but the correct path will only lead you to one.

▷ 5. Collect the token in that moon.

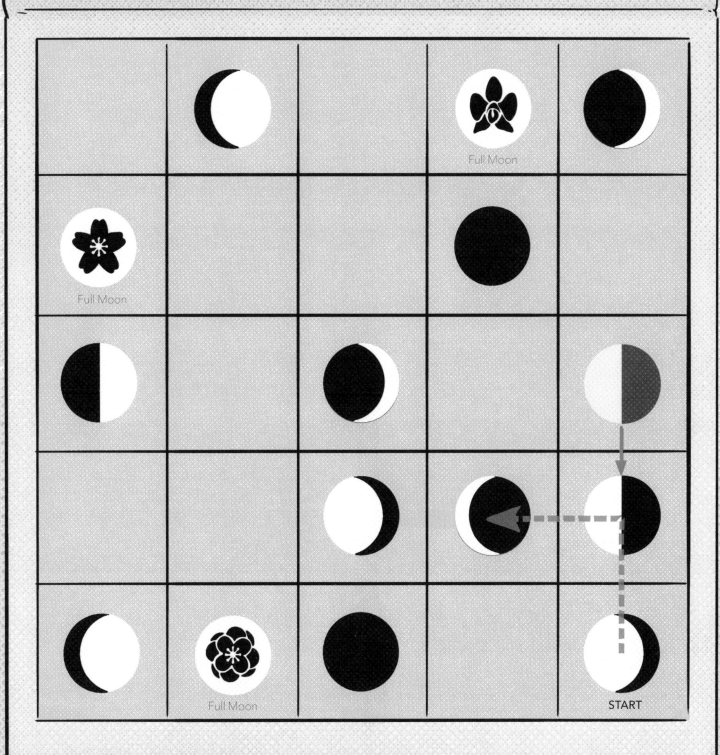

What do you want? I'm very busy.

Oh, er, we're on a mission to make sure the special exhibition can open tomorrow.

Humph. Well, I suppose that is quite important, but I've got far too much on my paws here already. The animals in the American Wing have had a huge argument and now I must figure out where everyone is going to sit. It's impossible!

Maybe if we help you with that, you'd be able to give us the token we need?

I don't think you can do it, but by all means, give it a try. Ready?

▷ The deer is already sitting in the correct spot and can tell you where the animals can and cannot sit. Use her statements to figure out the correct seating plan. "Next to" means up, down, left, or right.

▷ When you know where the animals can sit, match it to one of the grids below the seating plan and collect that token.

Are you OK, Ruby? I saw you fall in the reflecting pool, and I know you don't like water. Wowee, look at this! We're at the Temple of Dendur. Ancient Egyptian temples were built as houses for the gods. I can't see anyone here at the moment but there's a note from one of the curators.

William! I'm sorry to miss you but I had to dash. I know that you're in a hurry but if you can help me out maybe I can give you something you need for your quest. The temple is covered in carvings, and we need to count the ankhs. These are often held by the gods and symbolize life, and are also used as hieroglyphs in writing. You can use the drawing below to identify them.

▷ Once you know how many ankhs there are, collect the token that matches that number.

Ankh

Hello, William, how are you? We haven't seen you in the Islamic Art galleries for a while. Did you hear? The curators found five Egyptian fish amulets inside the stork's beak! We had wondered why she'd been so quiet. But anyway, I know you need some help. Perhaps we could do a favor for each other? I need to put these tiles together, but someone dropped the box and now they're all over the floor.

▷ **Can you figure out which set of tiles will complete the pattern? You might need to rotate them. Once you know which is the correct set, collect the token.**

Five fish amulets? I bet that ruffled some feathers.

We'd be happy to help you with those tiles! 'Alam Guman is especially good at putting things together. Let's see ...

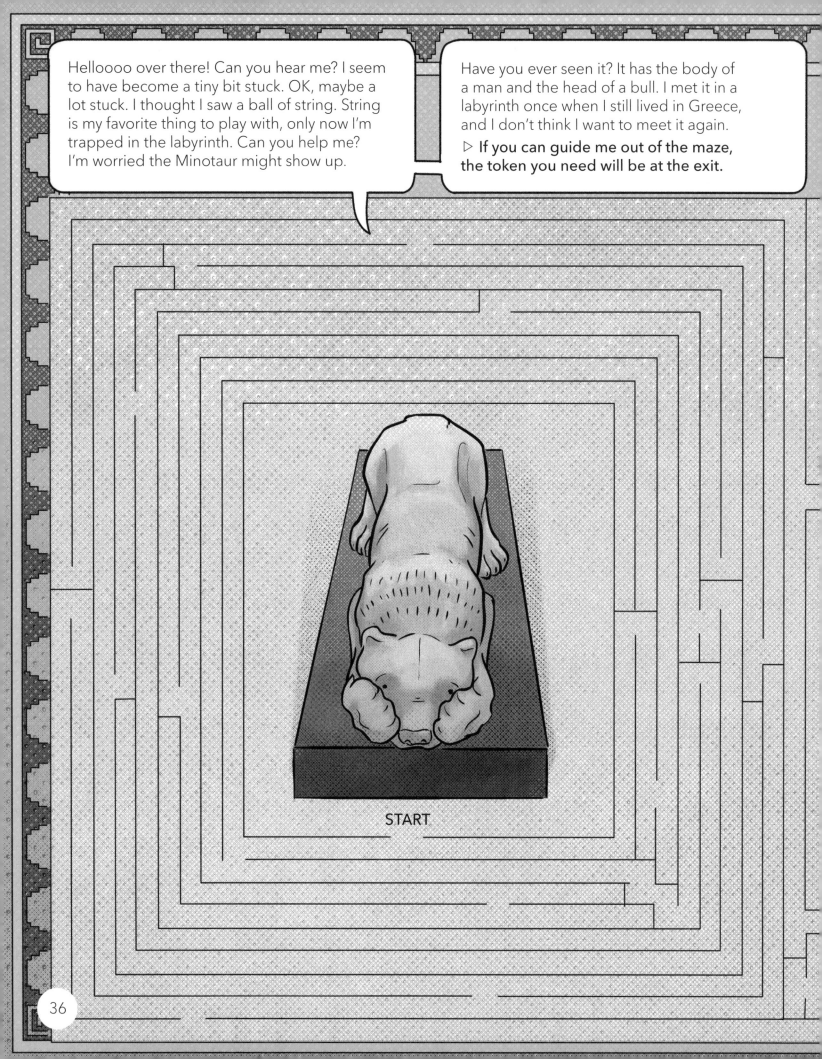

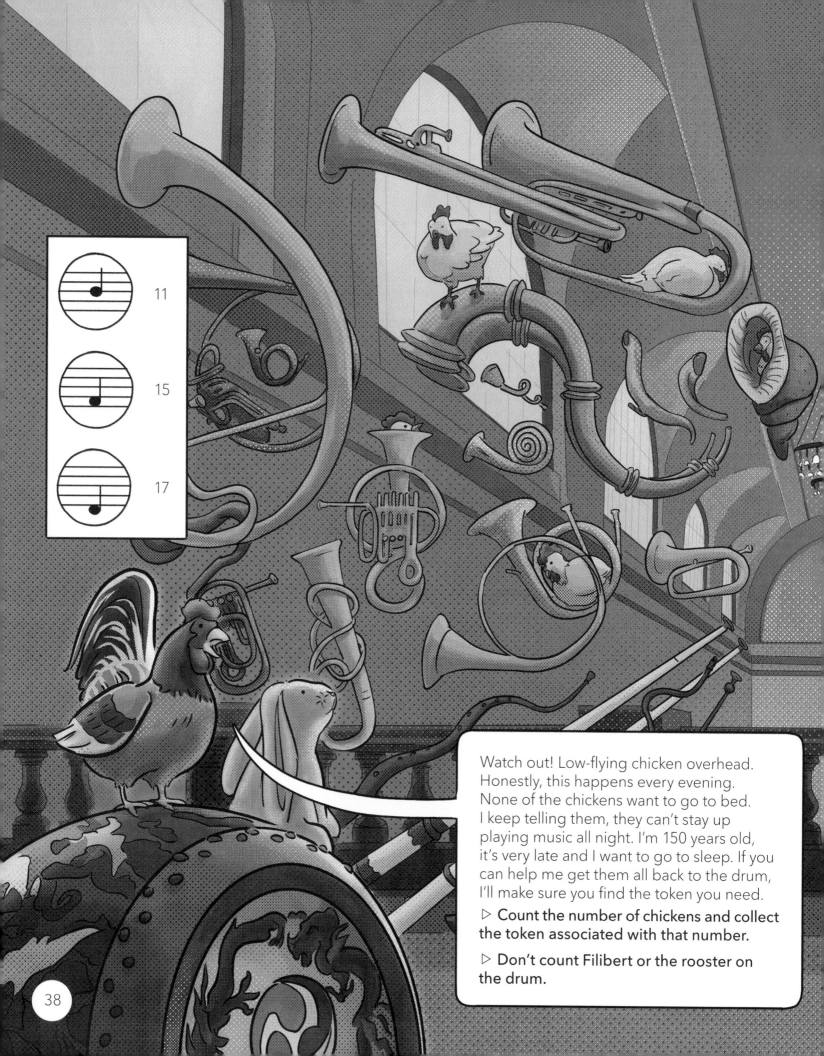

Watch out! Low-flying chicken overhead. Honestly, this happens every evening. None of the chickens want to go to bed. I keep telling them, they can't stay up playing music all night. I'm 150 years old, it's very late and I want to go to sleep. If you can help me get them all back to the drum, I'll make sure you find the token you need.

▷ Count the number of chickens and collect the token associated with that number.

▷ Don't count Filibert or the rooster on the drum.

This sounds like your dream job, Ruby—let's chase some chickens! But please don't eat any or I don't think we'll get the right token.

Hi William,

We've lost the department weighing scales—can you help us find out the weight of the purple-red cabbage?

The okra weighs 500 g.

The blue-green cabbage is twice the weight of the okra.

The crinkly savoy cabbage is 1/4 of the weight of the blue-green cabbage.

The Hubbard squash is three times the weight of the savoy cabbage.

The eggplant is 250 g lighter than the Hubbard squash.

The balsam apple weighs 10 percent of the weight of the eggplant.

The tomatoes weigh 100 g more than the balsam apple.

The purple-red cabbage weighs 400 g more than the tomatoes.

▷ When you know the weight of the purple-red cabbage based on the information above, collect the token that matches it. Grab a calculator and a piece of paper to help you figure it out.

T — 450 g

U — 550 g

R — 650 g

I've invented a new board game. It's based on a popular Egyptian game called Senet, but my version is a little simpler. If you help me test it out, I'll give you the hieroglyph you need.

These are the rules:

▷ Move from the start to the finish point, following the arrows around the board.

▷ To move, close your eyes and use your finger or the eraser end of a pencil and put it down on the number wheel. Whichever number you are pointing to, move forward by that many squares.

▷ If you land on a "good" square, then move two spaces forward. If you land on a "water" square, move two spaces back.

▷ Once you make it to the end, turn the page upside down to find your token. No cheating!

FINISH

Squaarrrkkk! What a mess! The donkey got loose, and some of the cogs fell out of the waterwheel. I must get it working as soon as possible. You're a clever bunch, can you help get it started again? BLUE cogs turn left, and RED cogs turn right. You'll have to put the correctly colored cogs in the correct place. Get it right and the water will rise from the well.

This is a tricky one, so let us make sure we understand it properly.

Blue cogs will turn to the left, or counterclockwise. Red cogs will turn right, or clockwise.

So, if you put a blue cog into the waterwheel, it will turn to the left and the next one along will turn to the right.

The cogs alternate until they reach the last one. To raise the water, the final cog must turn to the right. There are three sets of cogs pictured here but only one set will power the machine correctly.

▷ **Read the information above, then when you know which set of cogs is the correct one, collect the right token.**

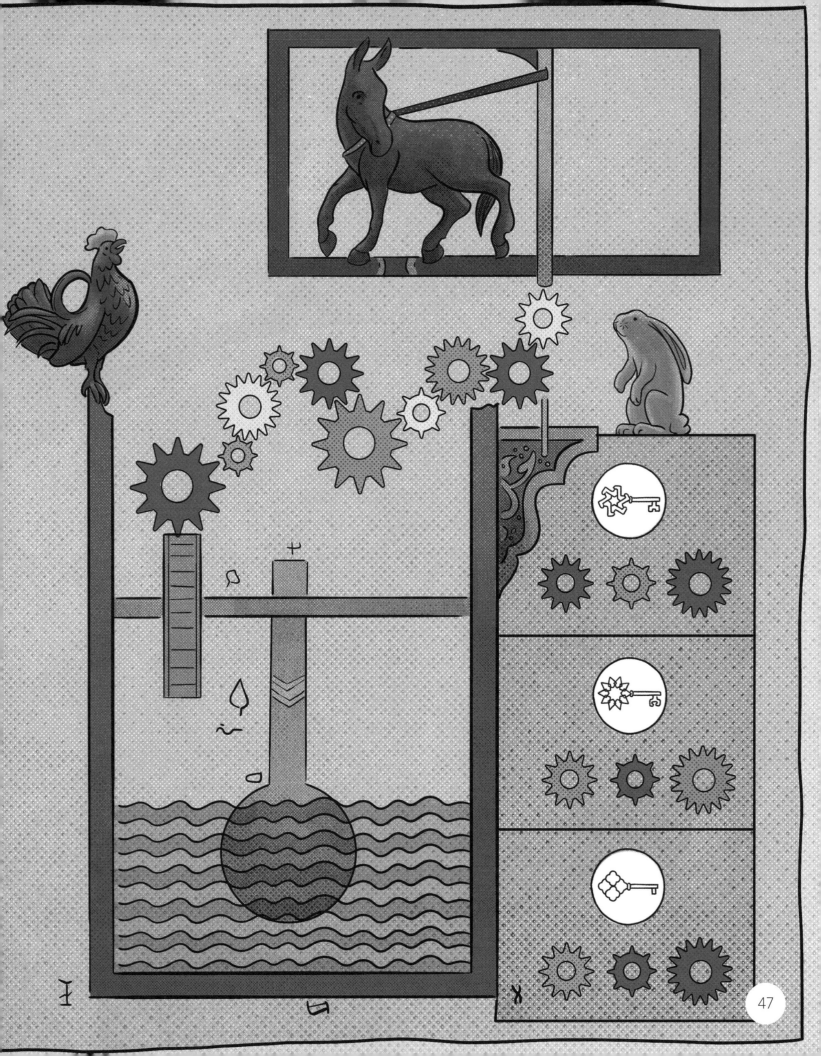

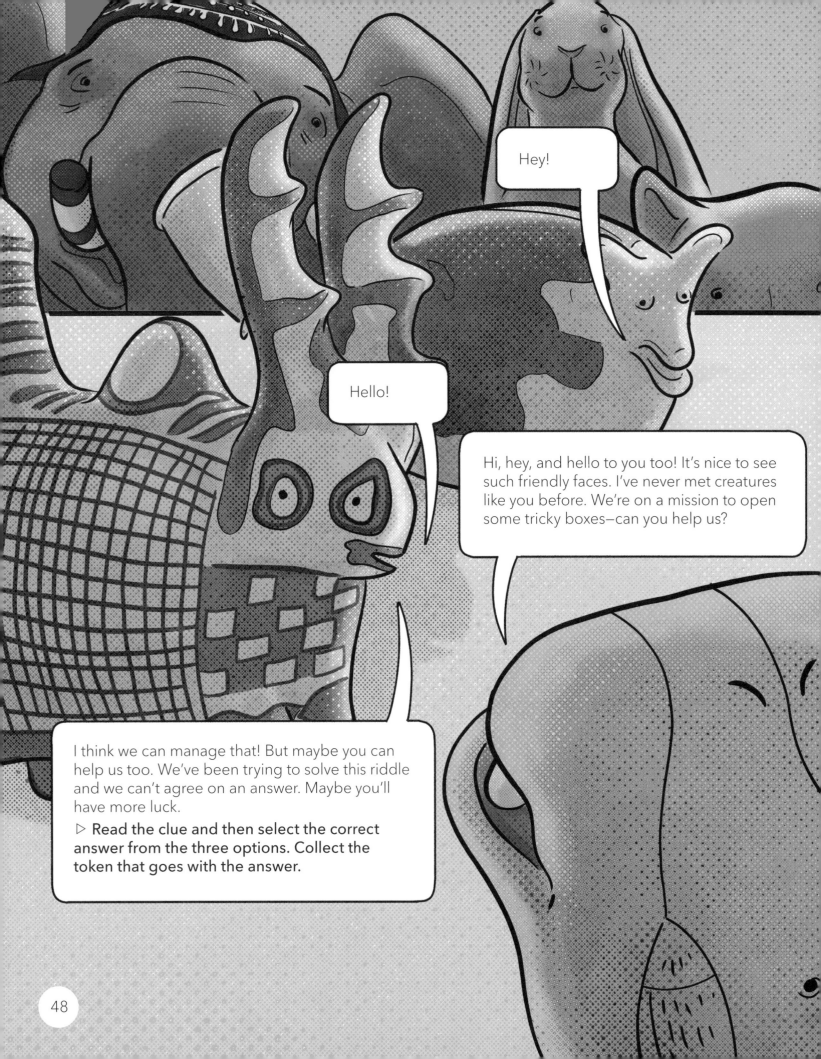

Hey!

Hello!

Hi, hey, and hello to you too! It's nice to see such friendly faces. I've never met creatures like you before. We're on a mission to open some tricky boxes—can you help us?

I think we can manage that! But maybe you can help us too. We've been trying to solve this riddle and we can't agree on an answer. Maybe you'll have more luck.

▷ Read the clue and then select the correct answer from the three options. Collect the token that goes with the answer.

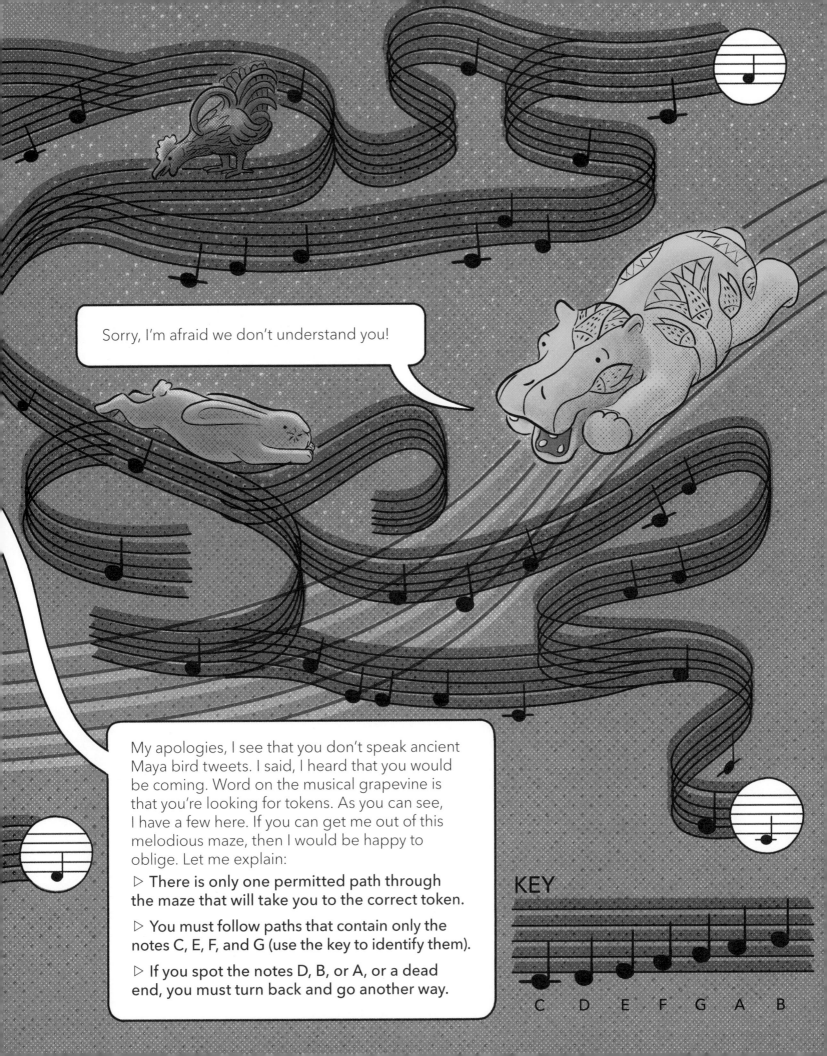

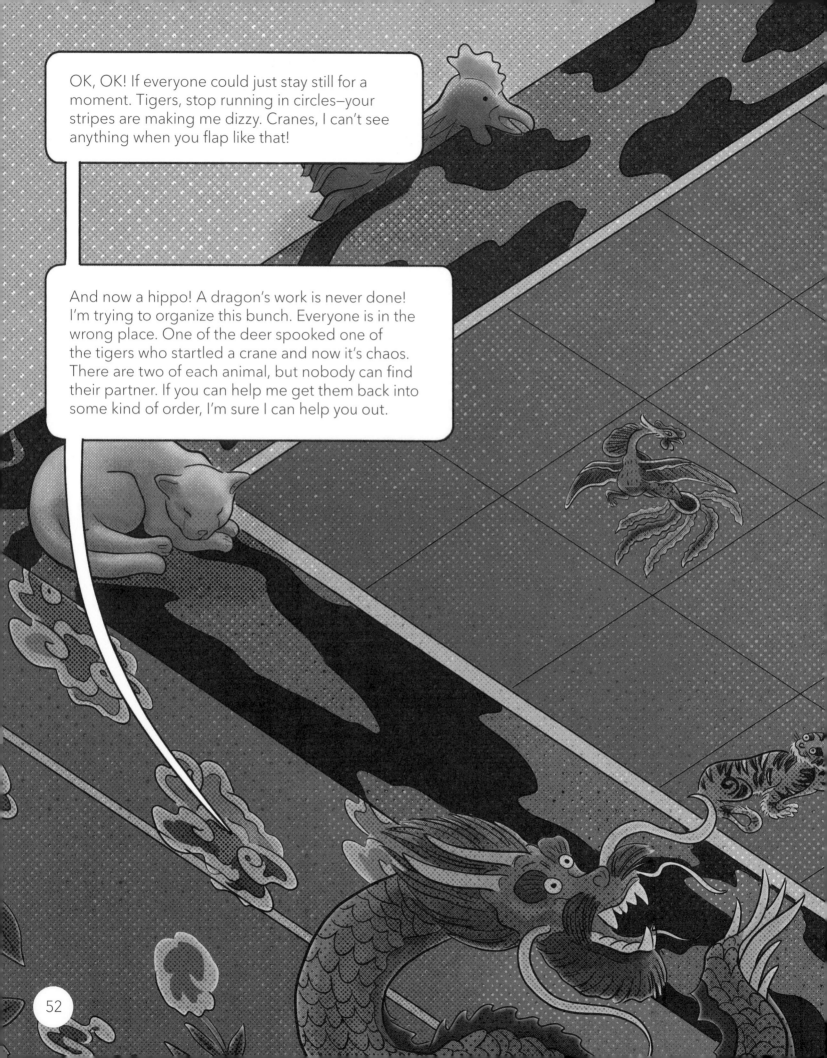

OK, OK! If everyone could just stay still for a moment. Tigers, stop running in circles—your stripes are making me dizzy. Cranes, I can't see anything when you flap like that!

And now a hippo! A dragon's work is never done! I'm trying to organize this bunch. Everyone is in the wrong place. One of the deer spooked one of the tigers who startled a crane and now it's chaos. There are two of each animal, but nobody can find their partner. If you can help me get them back into some kind of order, I'm sure I can help you out.

I've seen this kind of puzzle before! We need to match up the animals using the grid.

▷ Link the pairs to each other by traveling over the squares in straight lines. Use the shortest possible route between each pair. Do not travel diagonally or cross over another animal.

▷ When all of the animals have found their partners you can collect the token next to the animal with the longest path between the pairs.

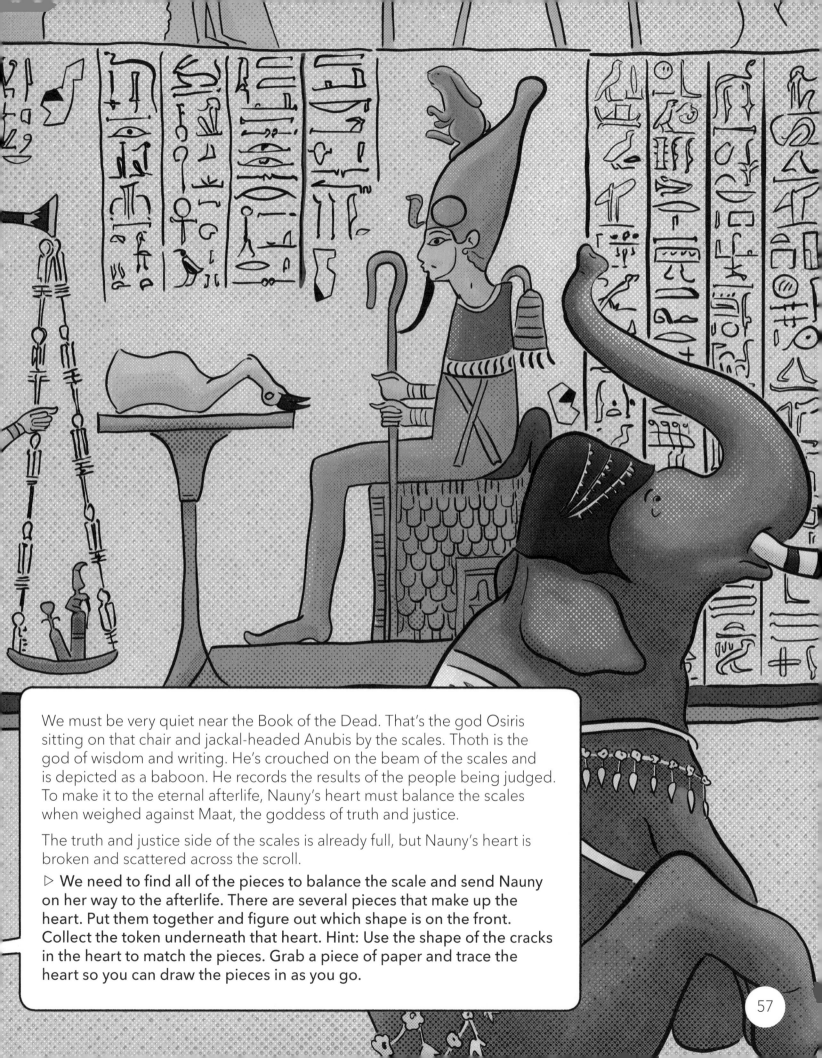

We must be very quiet near the Book of the Dead. That's the god Osiris sitting on that chair and jackal-headed Anubis by the scales. Thoth is the god of wisdom and writing. He's crouched on the beam of the scales and is depicted as a baboon. He records the results of the people being judged. To make it to the eternal afterlife, Nauny's heart must balance the scales when weighed against Maat, the goddess of truth and justice.

The truth and justice side of the scales is already full, but Nauny's heart is broken and scattered across the scroll.

▷ We need to find all of the pieces to balance the scale and send Nauny on her way to the afterlife. There are several pieces that make up the heart. Put them together and figure out which shape is on the front. Collect the token underneath that heart. Hint: Use the shape of the cracks in the heart to match the pieces. Grab a piece of paper and trace the heart so you can draw the pieces in as you go.

57

You've done it! And just in the nick of time! I've given all of the puzzle codes to the curators. The exhibition is ready for the grand opening—it's just through this door.

Oh no! It's locked! We've gotten this far; we can't let a locked door stop us from getting to the exhibition opening! One last puzzle and we're there. OK, let's see. The symbols above the door look familiar. Where have I seen them before? There's lots of information on the map; we could look there. I think we have to translate the symbols into numbers and type it into the keypad to open the door. Once it's open, turn the page!

Grab a piece of paper and write down the correct sequence of numbers.

What a wonderful surprise!
I knew there were other
hippos like me at museums
across the globe but I never
thought I'd see so many in
one place.

61

ANSWERS

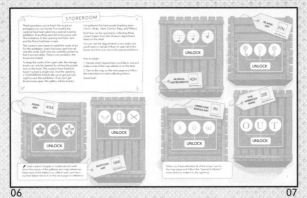

06   07

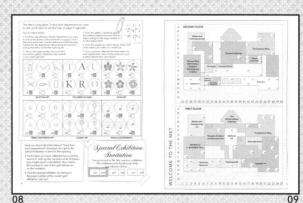

08   09

22   23

24   25

26   27

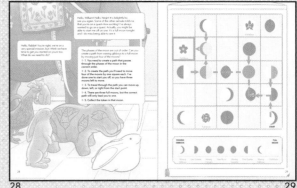

28   29

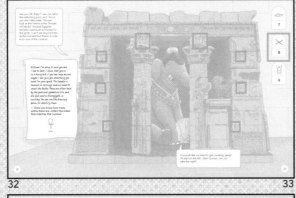

32   33

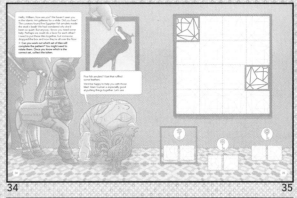

34   35

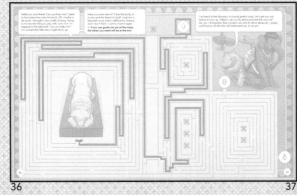

36   37

38   39

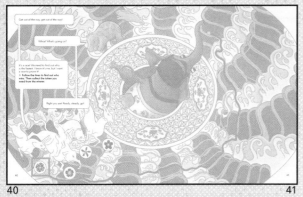
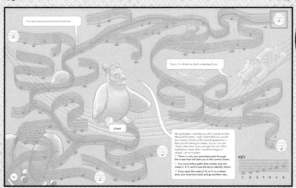
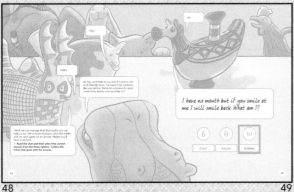

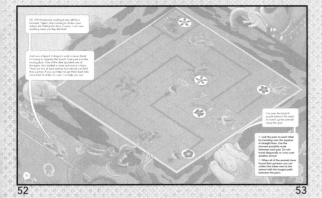

pg 42-43 The American Wing

(U)

Okra: 500g
Blue-green cabbage: 500 x 2 = 1000
Crinkly savoy cabbage: 25% of 1000 = 250
Hubbard squash: 3 x 250 = 750
Eggplant: 750 − 250 = 500
Balsam apple: 10% of 500 = 50
Tomatoes: 50 + 100 = 150
Purple-red cabbage: 150 + 400 = 550g

pg 30-31 The American Wing

(O)

Cat	Deer
Bear	Dog
Buffalo	Horse

pg 44-45 Egyptian Gallery

pg 58-59 Finale

1 7 9 1 1 2

Project Editor Rosie Peet
Project Art Editor Jon Hall
Art Director Giorgia Chiarion
Designer Vicky Read
Production Editor Siu Yin Chan
Production Controller Louise Minihane
Senior Acquisitions Editor Katy Flint
Managing Art Editor Vicky Short
Publishing Director Mark Searle

Written and illustrated by Helen Friel

Color and additional art by Ben Hooley

First American Edition, 2023
Published in the United States by DK Publishing
1745 Broadway, 20th Floor, New York, NY 10019

Page design copyright © 2023 Dorling Kindersley Limited
DK, a Division of Penguin Random House LLC
23 24 25 26 27 10 9 8 7 6 5 4 3 2 1
001–329257–Aug/2023

The Metropolitan
Museum of Art
New York

© 2023 The Metropolitan Museum of Art

Text and illustration copyright © Helen Friel, 2023

All rights reserved.
Without limiting the rights under the copyright reserved above, no part of this publication may be reproduced, stored in or introduced into a retrieval system, or transmitted, in any form, or by any means (electronic, mechanical, photocopying, recording, or otherwise), without the prior written permission of the copyright owner.
Published in Great Britain by Dorling Kindersley Limited

A catalog record for this book
is available from the Library of Congress.
ISBN 978-0-7440-6097-3

DK books are available at special discounts when purchased
in bulk for sales promotions, premiums, fund-raising, or educational use.
For details, contact: DK Publishing Special Markets,
1745 Broadway, 20th Floor, New York, NY 10019
SpecialSales@dk.com

Printed and bound in China

Acknowledgments
The author would like to thank the whole team at DK along with Ben Hooley and Kate Johnson. Thank you to all of the puzzle-testers and proofreaders, including Charlie Cochrane, Leo Parker, Dena Stock, Tali Stock, Greg Jones, Yoko Jarvis, and Ian and Lynne Friel.

DK would like to thank Stephen Mannello, Rachel High, and Laura Corey at The Met; the curators from Egyptian Art, Islamic Art, Asian Art, Greek and Roman Art, the American Wing, and Musical Instruments at The Met; Hilary Becker; Helen Friel; Giorgia Chiarion; Vicky Read; Rene Nel; Rica Dearman; Ben Hooley; Kate Johnson; Julia March, Lisa Stock, Jon Hall, and Tori Kosara at DK; and all the puzzle-testers.

Publisher's note:
The animals in this book are on a magical adventure in The Metropolitan Museum of Art. The objects in the Museum are all very precious, so if you go to visit the Museum in real life, be more careful than Ruby the cat and take care not to touch the objects.

The illustrations in this book are artistic renderings of Met objects and not intended as accurate replicas. Not all of the objects depicted in this book are always on display at the Museum.

For the curious
www.dk.com
www.metmuseum.org

MIX
Paper | Supporting
responsible forestry
FSC™ C018179

This book was made with Forest Stewardship Council™ certified paper—one small step in DK's commitment to a sustainable future. For more information, go to www.dk.com/our-green-pledge